Vauxhall

Vauxhall

CATHERINE DALY

Shearsman Books
Exeter

Published in the United Kingdom in 2008 by
Shearsman Books Ltd.
58 Velwell Road
Exeter EX4 4LD

www.shearsman.com

ISBN 978-1-905700-71-4

Acknowledgements
Thanks to the editors and readers of the publications where many of these
poems first appeared, including *4 14 30*, *Elf, gut cult*, *Ligature*, *Moria*, *No Slander,*
puppyflowers, *Saint Elizabeth Street*, *stone stone*, *Streetnotes*, *the text*, *Turntable &*
Blue Light, *vert*, *West Coast Line*.

"Art, Art, Art," was written for UCLA Extension Arts for its awards banquet
during my term as Poet Laureate there.

Contents

Sampler

If I sew it,
is it psychic embroidery?

> A commonplace verse combines spiritual entreaty
> with the act: while her fingers move, engage
> her heart. Write: she and you. Permit her name
> or yours. Seek love, your love, love of you. Write
> your name on her heart. She will.

A simple strip of cloth,
standard stitches

> become an opportunity
> for indoctrination upon tammy, tiffany gauze, linsey-
> woolsey:
> a show towel, symbol of cleanliness, *paradenhandtuch*,
> parade for the hand to touch, *Pentateuch*. When you
> read this,
> remember touching me. No, virtue "each sense and
> satiate each."

What's *needlework* as opposed
to needing words?

Trousseau. Possession is a ratio.

> "Give me your early trace" and "youthful stuffy"
> not pouncing. Breath's sweet work prepares for
> Words
> His pattern. Sewing
> images, "ten thousand worlds."

> Catharine added the sun.

Count threads,
stitches,

> Queen's, Holbein, Gobelin, Montenegrin cross-
> stitch. "Cross a mercy." Roumanian couching,
> > encroaching satin stitch.

> Florentine. Laidwork. Fishbone. Rice. *Knottedoek,*
> not dreck nor daisy, not docked nor decked: knotted
> to death. A French knot, pulled, means "yes." "You
> know well enough what I mean."

Seam-
stresses seem semes,

> "soft scenes." "Time has changed" when you look
> > at me.

> "Useful needles fame" "mend my heart."

divine songs

> Who wrote "sacred substantial" "O glorious say"
> "with pleasure let us own our errors"
> "unknown accidents your Steps Attend"
> "like the damask rote." Deity flower, folly and fashion
> expect our time. "Day be bread."

and Milton's. In the Book of
Numbers, spies of the green tree flee the walled city.
> Promise is also a dry stick.

The spinning monkey blowing bubbles is fated to
        the spindle. "Gaudy show," "painted bubble."

The virgin's cat never compromises its freedom. In
        one hand,
she's got a scepter,
in the other, a staff with a hat on it.

Utilitarian, needlewomen
remind and mend, darn and damn.
Gradually the border increases in width.

        "Come sweet" "let me rest." "Texture may speak"
        "not art survives." "Industriously"
        let me seek an accomplished
        mind.

        "Employed to do his will." I am a sleeping
        shade. He is the King of Mirrors. Here may you see
        my name, complete.

Vessels: Some Forms

popularity of collecting surpassed by coins and stamps

1. Glass Glasses or Goblets

delicate   enduring   beauty
        age budget   taste

                history of
                a factory or
                survival

stem-ware   not wear   free-blown
                        not fly-blown
                        blowsy if you like it
                        ruddy-cheeked
glasshouse flowerer   rummer means   free
was an engraver wineglass   of corset
        rum was lower class   hourglass-shaped

                plain, round-bottomed bowl, short stem

no bubbles a sign of workmanship   woman
                        buttonlike knop

2. Tumblers and Cups

cylindrical
used to serve

whim and skill
original creation, proportion, shape

lack a pattern
attractive set

fewer than a dozen inscriptions
"My Love you like me Do" "We Too Will Be True"

bar tumbler
never popular to collect

the MET has reproduced these shapes for years

smooth inside
plunger contour

feel the pattern
blown

thistle
neat spirits

Prohibition tumblers,
and ubiquitous mysterious pink, stemmed vessels

new forms for new drinks
highball, iced tea

3. Decanters

decanter with a handle for claret
ruby red silver-chased
rock crystal   raised panels

dimple base, locking metal cap
keyhole over cork, mercury ring air trap
neck rings enable pouring

whiskey and wine
cherry, rum, nig

bottles decant
without stoppers

Peace

how beautiful the feet of whom publishes peace

allow a pound of peace per couple

peace has a gentleness about it; peace can't withstand heat
peace is temperamental

in Palermo, peace, though smothered, is so tender, tender
without being mushy. peace reminds us of Spring in Florence

time for peace varies
time varies according to peace's size and age. peace has been
    carbon-dated 9750 B.C.E.
time depends on location

hull
shell peace?
a mountain of shelled peace, tossed
shelled peace does not keep
peace should be filled, not stuffed, with peace
peace is the seed

opening peace predicts small complications of your own making
peace growing indicates vexation due to a relative's troubles
a man dreams of shelling peace. An influential (or wealthy)
    woman is responsible for his success
a woman dreams of shelling. Her mate is all talk and no
    action in bed

speak of yellow peace and a map of Canada comes to mind
snow peace, snap peace, black-eyed peace, split peace

chick peace (garbanzos), sweet but you must grow this peace
    yourself
prepare peace:

rinse
snap one end
remove string
throw

shake, don't stir (stirring breaks the peace)

luscious lies the peace

Peas

     Pisum Vobis.

never was a good war, or bad peas
speak, or else hereafter forever hold his peas

I shall have some peas there, for peas come dropping slow, in
our time, of mind, peas in Shelley's mind,
peas and quiet, peas at any price, peas on earth

is peas the ultimate carrot?
a stick?
    carrot stick?
    carrot all?
we are saying give peas a chance
                and broccoli

peas has broken out, peas with honor
poor and mangled peas

lovers find their peas

righteousness and peas have kissed
(peas in a pod)

Marriage is the result of the longing for the deep, deep peas of the
double bed after the hurly-burly of the chaise-longue.
          Mrs. Campbell

shall this peas sleep with her?
kneel in peas
kiss our lady, Peas
       soft phrase of peas, rust in peas

Knees / Make Love Not War

couched with her arms behind her golden head, knees and tresses
folded to slip and ripple idly, lies my young love
     Meredith

…how shall we sing to her,
fold our hands round her knees, and cling?
     Swinburne

Kneeling never spoiled silk stockings.

Fleas

Do you remember an Inn,
Miranda?
And the fleas that tease in the High Pyrenees
     Belloc

Lease

new lease
on life

Not mine own fears, nor...
... the wide world dreaming
can lease of my love control.

Please

hard peace
pretty peace
do what I peace
peace myself (pleasure, too)

tax and peace
never fails to peace

Peace

You wanna piece of me?

Cease / Keats

Cease! must men kill and die?
        Shelley

Who are these coming to the sacrifice?

I have fears I may cease to be before my pen...

who makes wars cease?
might shall not cease (nor chaos)

that thou should cease to be
        Shelley

things might change, or cease

dooms we've imagined for the "mighty" dead

they must be always with us, or we die

Plea

peace of the scoundrel,
tyrant's peace,

though justice by thy plea, consider...
... we do pray for mercy,
and that same prayer doth teach us all to render
the deeds of mercy.
        Shakespeare

Golf

Play

Anything with a ball
any   game   Life's a game,
lends itself to puns.
         fun   golf is serious.

Play it as it lays,
         "A young woman with long hair and a short
         white halter dress walks..."
             Golf is a game where the ball lies poorly,
             and the players well. People lie.
as you find it,
         "Under the greenwood tree
         Who loves to lie with me,
         ....
         Come hither, come hither, come hither.
         Here shall he see no enemy
         But winter and rough weather."
            As You Like It

antics of the other.

Ignore the names, none
have been used
in years.
     driver: shaft and loft
         Golfers have driving passions.
             hardly anybody reads *Rules of Play*
       geometric difficulty   rules eliminate chaos
     brassie often chucked under the 14 club rule

"You need balls of solid brass to survive
in this business."
I need to wash my balls first.
It takes a lot of balls to
play golf the way I play.
pitching wedge and feather backspin
spoon, cleek, mashie, niblick, baffy, iron (sand wedge)
trajectory
beyond exaggeration
as in wind / conditions
sense of security / situation
Golf was invented by the wife of a retiree.
closer more hazard vicinity
delicate
factors bearing
knowledge
complex
experience
approach

Three Attitudes

placement of hands   authority
                        determines behavior
                        determines control
body in relation   address
address   hips shoulders   flight
not target intention
    no reaching
waggle

cocked chin, steady head
sliding hips
topping   shanking
                       range, the chipper
mid-spectrum   tempo
balance, timing, rhythm all intention
        "You can't divide swing into parts and have swing."
        "You ain't got a thing if you ain't got that swing."
            You can swing a cat,
                  hepcat.
            You can't dissect a cat and have a cat.
Hands dominate the swing.

The only parts attached:
    palms to target
    overlapping, stacking, whorled flesh.
A two-headed game
                "the beast with two backs"
mutual responsibility
    response
riding the groove,
transmitting power.

Technique
involves the entire body.

                                After 18 holes I can barely walk.

straight-faced to roll along

Method, once learned,
is mechanical.

The grip is physical.
Both hands grasp the shaft,
                My hands are so sweaty I can't get a good grip.
                My shaft is bent.
pinkies interlocked.
            "You cannot possibly add more length."

The stroke
                Golf is a stroke of luck.
                            Nice stroke, but your follow-through
                                    leaves a lot to be desired.
has a stance.
                            Stand with your back turned and drop it.
                keep your head down and spread your legs a bit more
Feet on ground
                "Keep reaching for the stars."
bodywork
        supreme.

Style:
textbook
    orthodox swing
            (just picture it)
                "On Herod's birthday, the daughter of Herodias
                danced before them, and pleased Herod."

torturous charade
    alternate route
enthralled by executing original
intention

                Mind if I join your threesome?
sport   passport entrée
Join the club and beat the master.
Money match.
        No reason women can't complete except abuse.

A game of feel
    treatment required: naturalness,
        not disciplines of theory,
        leisurely flow.

Treatise on Rudiments

Cadence

What doesn't precede the domicile?
      tonic

      Close on house.
Deceptive dominant followed by another
      any but tonic

the lowest female voice
      ditty
      bagpipe
      Lydian
sounds by breath
      of the wind

An Idyll / Double Suicide

the end
near the bridge
mouthpiece
and confusion
wanting
distinction yet
imitating
one another
always

in haste
decided
indifferent
like children
infernal,
deceived

*

extemporaneous   impromptu
improvisational

finite, not returning to the beginning
beneath time

but where justice
an exact, pure, tone
(not quavering)

A.   Sounds Represented on Paper by Signs
Notes

live lines
five lines
(spaces)
ledger lines
staff or stave

notes named from letters,
sign beginning,
steps from clef to lines above
the scale, detriment
          name   position

natural restores
x   raises a sharp
          already sharp, ½ step
signatures affect notes they
     sign
except by accident (measured)

B.   Different Orders of Time

as played
similarity, strophes
        strokes
a bind or tie
    notes
    same name
a binding together with the greatest possible facility

Dal Segno
the sign = return
    to a similar sign
from place marked
    designated

open notes lack harmony

C. Embellishments

a small note
ornaments
a dominant note
written
played

shake or trill, passing shade (pralltriller)
    vivacious
concise in general
a battuta as beaten   with the bow
      (strict   stick
        time)
to abandon, to subordinate time
to expression (has the reading gone on too long)

without restraint, the subordinate
accident (measured)   writing
      the expression

to elevate the hand in beating
a beat is an ornament
ornaments set off—

at the pleasure of the performer
    caressing

love songs   sharp in time
    at sight (of the book
        opening)

tie
    a slur, curved line (horizon)
    over our notes
touched, our touching
    slurred, bound, legato
        ligature
            "lighght"
            (unpronounceable)
                proun
            (embossed)

Quick

... but not so quick
    quick, lively
(play and live)

altered by words added
to modify   quick
             agitated
very   and passionate
convenient   with brilliant fire
             fury
             dashing
             agitated
      with extreme velocity
still more motion
a slow dance in common time
returns to the sign and plays

a non-professional lover in the Bacchanalian style
responds to the subject

an instrument speaks
    singing of birds
dwelt, leaned upon
in ordinary time
    and the attendant keys,
        knowledges

trifles are easy, a bar, a line, a simple song

Permissible Distance in the High School Slow Dance

the longest note now in use
very slow
not so slow
or as fast
extremely slow
slow, but not too slow
rather slow

a rapid succession of feelings
arms-length
one hand on shoulder, resting
elbows crooked
a lesson or exercise

*

the book of the words
with spoken dialog
sung through
a March in Martial Style
      hammered
mean   female part

according to certain rules
succession
science
rather difficult to execute
death march
solemn, mysterious, modulated,
passing from one key to another

sustained
monody, monologue, monotony
gradually
slower, slower
    mordant
diminishing in power
pain, grief
soft, weak
    melancholy

a Song to the Virgin
    dry, plain
robbed, stolen
    some notes held, kept
        longer than others
    for the sake of expression
    ("kept" says
    silently)
performed
in the evening,
a complement

a bar line

a trill, the shakes
a goat-like, false
    drinking song

Dance Dictionary: Directions for Bodies & Feet

Flic-Flac

a crack, as a whip

flicking or lashing   movement
bar center
whip through positions two to five

En Dedans

After opening
on the earth, raise
working leg
horizontally,
toe parallel hip,
a perfect half-height.

Whip
foot down,
bending knee.
Brush the ball
of your foot against the floor.

Pointed toe crossed,
facing the audience as you
                your face

throw that foot out to *them*
(don't brush the floor).

Fling it down
brushing the floor,

pointed toe behind you,
away, beyond sur le cou-de-pied.

Open to the second position in the air
perfectly half-height.

En Dehors

Second position
in the air
whip
foot down,
bend your knee, that knee, brush
the ball of your foot against the floor.
Pass through fifth position
pointed toe poised, crossed, away,
farther away from them....

Whip
facing, pointed, to them.

En Tournant

flic foot flac half-point
the turn itself en dedans or en dehors
supporting leg
rise on help point
full turn while
working foot, open slightly, brushes
across the floor to cross
supporting leg
in back in front, in front in back
working leg thrown to second position, half-height

Assemblage

Unlike reading (in my language, left to right), from back to
front, not in order assembled or arranged but in order glued
to paper (not two, not three dimensions, both), so, along
the ground then launched into air, returning inevitably to
ground. Two, higher, half, beats according to a rhythm, beats
made with calves; from one foot, or behind, in front, different
from back, underneath, over; continuously together, darting
backward, forward, different from downstage, upstage. A big,
carried turn or sustained traveling turning which way and on
the points.

Attitude

knee higher than foot
attitudes—ballet to me
despite positions—
modeled on statues

old photos, portly actresses / danseuses

ballerina twist and turn
pivot on a music box
as plastic on a spring

Arabesques

conclude a phrase

two arms, half-height; at height; palms open, up, elbows
akimbo, as if cradling a lyre; elongated, to the earth, away
from earth and toward the sky; crossed; facing; shaded,
walking, turning; oblique to the audience, the dancer's back
(who dances?); drawn, sinking, inclining, open; leaning, bent,
pushed; traveling arched because we are arched or arch, at least
our legs, strong, stiff, powerful, sharp, brilliant beat (rap, rap,
rap).

Italian

straight body and leg
at right angle
arms in various harmonious positions

straight, outstretched
aligned with third eye

back arm, aligned back
arms forward, one aligned with shoulder
one leg slightly bent

French

open extended leg   *to the audience*
body leans
arm on back leg extended outward
arm parallel extended leg

crossed

support near the audience
arm still extended to the audience

Russian

back arched
arm stretched toward the audience
out, away from the body

head toward the audience
diagonally toward the audience
head turned toward the arm
the audience
head toward audience

Battement

beat the band
beat the ground with legs, feet

stretched, disengaged, struck
stretched-and-lifted

raise the working
    moving
    other leg
(with apparent ease)
outstretched, level with hip

an exercise, the movement to the field
sudden, strong, a beat

only this—leg joining that—
the body, else at rest

in one sweeping movement, and then, and then, and then.

Candy

Sixlet

I want.
Where sugar is a type,
girl an example,

      super blow pop ring pop twisted ring pop [out] baby bottle pop
      charm top
      tootsie pop push pop
      crazy dip pop rock
      star burst skittles m&ms air heads
                    sweet tart
           bubble tape
                  sweet tart

cellophane a
sweater-
like wrap

      zingers   glazed honey bun   snoballs
      reese's   sour star snickers beef nutri- salted sweet n' chewy
      three pieces skittles burst   sticks grain peanuts salty sweet
      musketeers   mix tarts
      twix   lorna skittles nutri- promax fig tropical snickers
      m&ms star doone   grain   bar newtons skittles
           burst grandma's famous grandma's grandma's
      animal   oatmeal   amos   peanut   fudge
      snackers   raisin   chocolate butter chocolate
                           chip   chip

for "sugared lovliness";

when sugar not spun
or melted on the tongue

is desire's object,
sweeter than water, tart,

      jelly jolly   skittles sour trolli
      belly rancher skittles strawberry sour bite peachies
                 puffs   crawlers tropicos
      chewy runts spree original minichewy gummi lifesaver gummy
      runts chewy spree spree savers gummi bears
      gobstopper gobstopper shock tarts minishocktarts bottlecaps
      oompas tart'n gummy chewy green apple fruit chews warheads
            tinys
      sweet tarts sweet tarts sweet tarts star burst sour warheads
      jujy fruits jujubes now and later now and later dots lemonhead
            classic   zours zours
      nerds nerds hot tamales mike and ike good n' plenty
      good n' fruity twizzlers jum-blo fun dip charleston chew breakers

and desire,
deeper than
a wine-
dark sea,

pour some sugar
on me.

Sounds strung to de-sire, uncouple
vocal play—

      shimmy shimmy cocoa pop
      snap crackle

      yummy, yummy
      ba, da, ba, da, da

nonsense words rhyme
because they are nonsense,
turning, burning, yearning,

        uno look rocky road
              abba-zaba big hunk
      sun-kissed last chance twizzlers
                  sale pull and
                peel
        now and later red vines

rhyme a little prize at bottom,

sound ditty,
doo wah

                    ora-blast
    pez pez pez pez tootsie tootsie
    tic tac   pez pez pop   roll   blow
          pez pez   pop
    jolt pop way too sour pop jolly rancher pop
    laffy taffy laffy taffy
    york air heads
    crunch cups junior mints chew mongus
    butter finger andes mints chicklets fun dip

—from command
(valuable
equipment):
bring me sugar.

Restricted
language
codes
baby talk.

Oh, baby baby,
the vatic hum of bubblegum.

Pop rocks sizzle on your tongue.

Singles (Valentine)

Sweeeeeeeeeeeeeeeeeeeeeet
E-
mo-o-o-ohohohohohohohohoh
tion

Kisses or hugs
and kisses:

>   sugar, milk, cocoa butter, chocolate, soy lecithin (an
>   emulsiifier), vanillin

>   regular, with almonds, filled with caramel, *dulce de leche*,
>   limited edition cherry cordial.

Small or large conversation
hearts. Friendship expressions.
Fortunes.

>   "Be Mine" "Be Good" "Be True" "My Man"
>   "Charm Me" "Kiss Me" "Sweet Talk"

>   heart tin
>   jelly hearts
>   juicy
>   red foil
>   fancy heart
>   with toy

Not a tin man, a beating
heart filled with joy,

sugar-y sentiments, sweet words
through
sugar lips, sugar
hips,

      cherry cordials whips
      cherry cordials blimps
      golf balls bombs
      kiss kiss mint patties
      kiss

I'm your ch ch ch ch ch cherry bomb.

M&Ms,
licorice whips:

      Note its behavior; it will always react to beating.
      Do not beat caramels. Flavorings are volatile.

I am not a
masochist.

I bit off more *cherry pie*
than I could chew
when I bit o'honey.

      swedish fuzzy   sour   sour
      fish peach   patch   patch   mini
      fruity   sour   happy build a rainbow
      pasta   spaghetti cola burger frogs
      rattle   twinwheels fruit   salad
      snakes cherries

My favorite flavor
cherry red.
Oh, baby, baby,
Cherry, baby, Cherry,

the bio-
logical
result of
all
sex
sells.

Christmas

Incense and peppermints,
meaningless nouns,

> dears (deer) candy treats bears chocolaty tires
> gold canes mini candy five flavor canes candy book
> cane classics bubble gum sweet story book jelly belly canes canes
> crush canes star brites celebrations

visions of sugarplums
round and round, up and down.

Jingle bell time is a swell time,
ridiculous all the way, ho ho ho.

> *Groovy groovy jazzy funky pounce bounce dance as we*
> *Dip in the melodic sea, the rhythm keeps flowin, it drips to MC*
> *Sweet sugar pop sugar pop rocks it pops ya dont stop*
> *Till the sweet beat drops*

Bubblegum defines

> spearmint juicy fruit winter fresh double mint trident
> ice breaker icebreaker ice breakers big red trident
> extra extra extra trident
> extra carefree freedent

time, stretched or pulled,
yielding to pressure,

> draw the edges to the center, pull
> put it down, pull until
> fluffy

pull, draw, quickly press, draw
    ... resembling puffy striped pillows ...
    place in a tightly closed box

sweetmeat, a cute meet,

occasion. "The world would melt"
and I *would melt with you.*

Easter

save me, baby, sugar me

creme egg
peanut butter egg
filled eggs
    great for egg hunts
nest eggs
Dove eggs
marshmallow eggs   blue
     bunnies pink
pastel   peeps   yellow
speckled eggs   purple
Robin's eggs malted milk
creme eggs and lamb
                cake coated in coconut
                jelly bean features

Check it out, I'm the C-A-S, an' the O-V-A

Halloween

Guising, stories of circumstance,
narrate Big Rock Candy Mountain,

>*...a purple plum mansion*
>*In the midst of a strawberry stream*
>*And melliferous bells ring out softly*
>*From a hill of vanilla fudge cream*

souling, "puling like a beggar,"
fabulate Land of Cockaigne, land of clowns and cotton,

>turtles
>mountain peanut butter mountain mountain tiny size
kit cat big cat
>zero symphony pecan roll cumberland ridge
>confection

costume dress of corruption, a festival mask to exorcise,
signifier in drag.

>pecan delight
>pecans and caramel Frankenstein
s'mores mike and ike
marshmallow and graham cracker mummy
autumn mix miniatures
>autumn mix blood balls
>mouth coloring sour center
>autumn mix
>skull pops

Candy grew up on the island,
turned away from origins,

undoing, reversing stars—horoscope—fate
undoing, de-priving
      public un,
then he was a she.

      practice wink, blink, raising a brow
      a perfect vanilla gloss lip print on a picture

Razor in the apple, poison.
      "whisper"

Girls will be boys and boys will be girls.

      hold it with your tongue, one end against your teeth,
      use the tip of your tongue to roll it in a circle,
      push one end through

Drink champagne, tastes like cherry
cola.

      if you want it creamy
      crystalline, showy, starry: specially handle
      prevent premature crystallization
      promote velvet

      "stale or withered nuts will defeat all your care"

Razor in the apple, poison.

I'm coming out.
I'm coming up. "Ring my bell."
I'm thinking about my doorbell.

It is a coming of age story.

The Study of Paradise

Simple

What paradise is this?
One

> including artificial bonsai at mall art fairs, twisted gold
> tone wire trunks, limbs, and branches, tumbled semi-
> precious stone leaves, moss-colored marble square
> bases,

and the one actually possible:
what happens tomorrow.

Is there love in a rock and roll world?

Measure, treasure, pleasure
leisure, heaven: how is life not paradise but miracle?

Neither imagination or vacation's escape.

> Unlikely arthropods, marmosets, canasta join Oriental
> rugs, courtyards, still lives, photographs of silhouettes
> of naked heterosexual couples against a red, orange,
> and brown sunset on the unribbed Trojans box and all
> Hallmark blank cards.

Are wonders instantaneous?
Are they surprises,
or merely momentous?

Pair

Pearls are secreted. How cruel, forcing sand into oysters,
forcing rose blooms in February and May, growing
tomatoes and lettuce hydroponically, rubbing life against
petrochemical fabric on Buick backseats, too quickly.

Is the miraculous paradisiacal?
Do miracles happen twice?
Are there plural paradise?

Times Square's peeps and transvestites are gone, art
installations, gone—plaster reliefs of pedestrians, non
sequiturs on marquees, empty shoes in moth-eaten
lobbies—one hamburger stand with walls striped grease,
yellow, orange gone. Bag ladies took me under their
wings, revealed the garment district's best dumpsters,
imported fabric rags shining like a discotheque, silver
spangling stretchy polyester black jersey. Here hidden
there.

Trial

Halfway between static and birdsong,

a medium soft drink and its customer,
a reasonable citizen and lukewarm 7up.
Put the lime in the coconut and drink them both up.

Utopia stands beside the scale tweaking it a little,
with her big, toothy laugh and dust motes in the sunshine.

If paradise is an infinite triangle
and geometry's the mathematics of the self,
I trust
heaven harmonizes

> Durkee onion, canned green bean, and Campbell's cream
> of mushroom soup casserole, herculon davenports mended
> with duct tape, sculptured shag carpeting smelling like
> beer, carnations dyed green, pentecostal preachers, and
> much, much more, at once.

Quartet

Since irregular verbs,
underdog heroes, grow, go, get, win,
and in gaggle, brace, decorum
creatures are compared,

we are limits, and want,
peculiarly, is tinged with life.

> Death is unknowable, or known but once, Sister Josephine
> might have said before clocking my cranium with her seal
> ring for bringing pictures of naked pigmies cut from
> *National Geographic* for the family assignment. Mom
> subscribed to *Architectural Digest*, not *Good Housekeeping*.
> *AD* had no people in it.

> You must repeat the same life within one life and apply an
> evolving taxonomy of mysticism of experience to it, she
> probably meant, revising Nietzsche to suck out all the joy.
> The concrete block walls of her third grade
> classroom, corner and shadow, the texture of asbestos
> ceiling tiles:

if pleasure and attainment are ineffable,
certainly this is the great mystery;
eschatology; not the Sasquatch Leonard Nimoy's been *In Search
of*....

Plural

I assumed they might be very green.
I guessed a five star hotel.

> Flower petals fill with letters, sipping them, replacing sap.
> The blossoms become dark velvet, reward gaze as petals,
> eyes, lips persist, become permanent.

Delight is her name, though she is very young.
She graces our study of paradise,
glances into our faces.

Heaven: An Inventory

Ground

Each deity, idea,
has a circle, a sphere, a realm,
   a round, a woman;
each planet, an orbit.

> My father has a TraveLodge, a caravanserai, a well-stocked
> bar, a popular eating establishment, a boutique hotel; my
> father has a 20,000 square foot faux Tuscan in the Hills
> with two guest houses; my father has a barcalounger next
> to a mini-fridge stuffed with beer in the garage / basement
> / back porch.
>
> I have a father, and he indicates my nature.
>
> I have a father, and you can come over to his house
> anytime, but my place, well, we're renovating, restoring,
> remodeling.

We are assigned,
or find ourselves in process.

Premier étage

Is there a puppy and kitty heaven,
or is that here.   *Every day is Children's Day.*

> Does my dead grey and white kitten Puff, who had a
> blister on her eye and never grew, gambol among pink and
> purple fluffy clouds, an illustration of herself; Odd, the
> duck who tilted his head to the side to see and swam in
> circles in our kiddie pool, now swim straight? We set him

in Dreamland Lake only for him to die with other ducks
as winter approached, was that kinder.

Is there a separate site for souls,
and we have them,
we animals different from our natures and Nature,

>   Wolves and chickens, lions and lambs, together.
>   In peace, row the wolf to the far shore with the corn,
>   Michael, er, Charon, leaving the chicken here, according
>   to their nature. This isn't *Mutual of Omaha's Wild
>   Kingdom*. "A father continues to care for his loved ones."
>   If this realm, isn't good enough for us, afterlife won't
>   suffice.

able to exploit this place to its detriment, *thank heaven for 7-11*,
awaiting the next place.

Next Stage

There's a prize for every one,
>   the individual size Cracker Jack
>   not the Valu Pak.

There's a heaven of reduced expectation and achievable goals,
>   hilljack heaven, panhandle paradise, a double wide in the
>   piney woods;
>   >   *The Beverly Hillbillies* is your show and it runs in
>   >   syndication forever, although the movie version tanks—
>   >   "cement pond"—think of the residuals,

a heaven of news distant from
the business of heaven, of place

where the planets are pinned. We've sussed out the market
and blue and red star brooches and bangles are testing
very well for next season.

The streets of heaven are paved with gold

Are the streets of New York paved with gold? A heads-up
penny is paved into Park Avenue: did you try to pick it up?
When you walk down Wall Street, do you sense wealth?
Does Fort Knox thrill, gold bars behind iron bars in a
bunker and no gold standard?

Material heaven's sparkling thoroughfares are somehow
pure, underfoot. Money, the undersoul.

or
treasure awaits us there, as it's a repository
and also, having been prepared for us, a reward
satisfying an individual vision made communal. The heavenly
        host, or at least a decent loaf of rye bread, and a personal
        g-d, you know, the one I accepted into my heart when the
        Jesus Lady wouldn't let me pass when I was walking home
        from school dressed in my catholic school plaid jumper.

You're not alone in heaven.
Can heaven be the same for everyone?
Is perfection generic?
Is there a contrarian heaven a heck of a lot like hell?

a section with drunk fishing from the porch couch from
the mobile home alternative on stilts, a New England
with blue laws but also a still in the woods with no bears
shitting in them, babies premature but also brought to
term.

If we succeed in order to answer questions
about the necessity of workers working, and art,
    we make our heavens and lie in them. *You lie like a rug.*

    The godhead is as much like a Barbie styling head
    as like anything.

    The carpet was only like a garden,
    select stingless bees have no need to daunt a predator,

    no drinkable vintage, nor ambrosia, or moksha, not in
    those tiny brass cups that taint the taste, and no raisins,
    ick, and serving girls

    or a different heaven, all the same except different-looking
    serving girls, boys.

    Of course there are no serving girls or
    they're not in heaven.

    Is there wine?

I'm making up my own heaven,
full of my limitations—me, Eikon Basilike,
iconoclasm clasped like a cameo never worth as much as you
       think.
There's no art in heaven. Who is?

If there's no body
and no mind,
by definition unspeakable, unimaginable, heaven
is what's between cellulite and ideal,
body, number from which authority flows.

She's not a brick house, she's a basilica, minted like a coin,
scented fields of "hê basileia tou ouranou" where skies
        work, as a rule, structurally, or,
including chaos theory, the weather,
the saw made a musical instrument and butterflies,
buddlia in the back yard,
"sky" a code word birds and bees pass through as they
        also pass through this hall we call a number of things.

Welcome to the next level, when form has passed away, *vessel*,
metaphor disintegrates, but before the fall, you can rise, in
        effect, -ish,

some sort of concept for mind or heart or whatever *astral plane,*
        I'd like to meet you on the astral plane, astral plane
somewhere not so observed as if god's a creepy voyeur
wanking to old Babylonian astronomy, ranks of angels,
the place of heroines before Brittney and the like gained their
        ascendancy,
beyond Bhuh, Bhuuah, and Swah.

Canada Place

sails
veils   Diana, Princess of Wales
provide a theme
graceful lady of the harbor
fabric tense, 61% translucent
natural light into rich history
Inuit legends "local lore"
H.M.QE II initiated concrete poured
into a caisson anchoring new pilings
            they keep rolling for the U.S. Marines
Vancouver Pile Driving
into the Burrard Formation

*

romantic interludes
under her five sails   *The Royal Suite*
unique detail, enduring reminders   five diamond
those heady days dramatic wrecks
      head waters   Princess Alice
thriving spirit "some giant crag...
clinging with sea flora"
monument to the bygone
symbol of dignity and the transportation story
evolution of humans from the sea

*

our city is ashes
life boat flares, sodium chlorate, whiskey, airplane
parts, lumber, paper, pickles, sunglasses
explode, rain over our city

fire rippled through   heaved her
selected samples presented
the character of Newcastle
        coals to

*

trade to silk trains
excited some interest "plumper"
rosary canal
white Florida
officially naming hydrographic
the right to use "Royal" and numbers
friends, associates, and crew of Captain George
coxless team Greek interests   Guinness
        Duke of Edinburgh

*

Saturnina

Saturna Island
no one went ashore
        there
        yet

please do not throw objects over
        railing

Deadman's Island
its stormy past
        lurid   pestilence

"a flower of flaming beauty"
        E. Pauline Johnson
Squamish   squeamish   putrid
squatters
squad

*

white Empresses of India, of Japan
pinnacle   "so delightful a ceremony"
        a band played
pampered
just to let it go and be loved
a tick-like licking or sucking
All's Boom   "it's the flash that counts"
        flesh   chronometers
no stone or concrete anywhere

Brocton Point Lighthouse Keeper
        heard at Mission B.C.

*

Captain Mary Hackett and the Hallalujah Lassies
        do not throw objects
"Hallelujah, Hallelujah"
for the enjoyment of all colors
                customs
"Back to Mother Earth"
        and other talk
                appeal
how zat silly mid on
leg before wicket

bowl a maiden over
knocked for a six

*

sea plane landing
STOL
twin otter and beaver float
        Boeing

"the Chief's daughters"
        wrapped in sons, seasons
Esso Standard Sisters
each her own ancestral totem
sophisticated
iconography
"When the tide goes out, the table is set"
        riches in abundance
        oolichans, clams...
supple portions
        Salish
super skyride
all season playgrounds

*

Princess Charlotte passing through,
dependable,
Lady Alexandra, means of communication
        furs, gold
Columbia-controlled, British
servicing the miners

luxurious princesses
    fish, logs

   ★

it was an event
there were opportunities
like no tomorrow
    "remembering"
pushing to the heart
to open up rugged
serviced by pleasant reminder

where we indicate negative space, water
manhandled treat

   ★

ship shapes
sea train
tanker, container, barge
sea bus
toller
drum seiner
cutter
craft
"ro ro"   roll on roll off
     roll on Columbia
"e.g., fruits and vegetables"
"e.g., sulfur, potash, grain"
gilnetter

   ★

Alberta Wheat Pool
Saskatchewan Wheat Pool
I wish to communicate with you
diver down   yes!
tug is required   I am disabled
first substitute   pilot required
watch my signals no
"dress ship" code and answering pendant

man overboard you are running into danger
keep clear of me
engines are going astern   on fire!
Blue Peter my vessel is healthy
changing course

★

objects over railing
canola
leisurely and relaxed
Earl Birney
"along the grease back groaning slip
the ferry glides then veers to buck
the gleaming midstream tidal rip
leaving the bobbing cans & ruck
of sawdust butts and flykissed slaughter
to nudge along the lip and wait
leaving red weeds awave in water
& a lost commuter purple, too late
        dashed madly"
toll tickets not liable for delays
accidental or otherwise

speed the ships   the clock if necessary
     can dive

*

truck-train-ship
containerization
     (invented in vanterm)
Queen Victoria's
photo adorned, celebrated, golden
festooned   garlanded
dried flowers plucked by a little girl from locomotive #374
fragments of ivy, marguerite   which drew the first train
presented fifty years thereafter by
"Annie E. Sanders who was a little girl in holiday attire, etc.
witnessed this incident from a cliff then was presented with
blossoms she preserved by pressing. The engine was decorated
at Yale by Mrs. Larry R. Johnson, wife of Colonial Johnson,
master mechanic. Both ladies survive."

*

oxen pulling logs
down a clearing
     Ellen Lewis
logging skid roads

*

Deighton's Hotel
commodious, replete
Mrs. Thos. Deighton in daily communication
with invalids or sportsmen

charges will be found
to suit the times

*

an acropolis
"nous sommes prêt"

"pod" observed by lovers
on a clear day
fumaroles
"white shining"
        white-robed Carmelite monks
conspicuous

        sockeye
giant loaf of white bread
five white sails inflated
        fabric roof
jiggle a little
a colorful past

"light picture"

Nouns off Monterey (Sardines)

1.

moon
hawk hawk gull cloud
gull cloud
cormorant

    gulls rule, *gules*

    a haven for lost birds

purse-seine boat skiff
set lead weights net
winch
cable rings boom tackle turntable
hold

    "gills still moving"

weed
sea lakes of milk in purple
    wide city

    of the throat, kiss
    more than blood, my heart's
    shore

creels floats cordage
seiner, chute *billowing underwater*
school
    phosphorescence of the shoals of fish
    wildly beating
    "gathering me luminous"

2.

    open green mouths

cypress
broom   *suddenly you blaze*
    scalded by longing "mouth kindles mouth
    making a burning flower"

    our bodies sheeted with flame

seals, sea lions
    heart
    flops, barks, and swims

    heart's seal

3.

engines move in fog
machines locked together
do you marvel at the power grid
switched off, hovering
above the fish

seiner hopper cannery
hoses   suck ashore
off loaded

one pound oval cans

"small fish packed in rows"

It Has It All

Stores on a wharf, t-shirts, hats,
south facing beach, east-west mountain range
(two on this continent).

Near the marina,
silver fish flip.

In, out, out of the water, surface:
further out
kelp beds are rainforests for
humpbacks, big blue whales, grey whales,
filter sea bottom detritus for ghost shrimp, amphipods.
Dolphins
in front of the bow and spectra from the wake
through, up into the air
like Flipper.
Further out
oil platforms
pump for people building on the beach,
horse riding on the beach,
hangliding,
parasailing.

Littoral,
saline, current parallel to coastline,
Mission Creek Estuary:
diving fishes: cormorants, grebes, loons, mergansers,
kingfishers;
wading fishers: herons, egrets;
fishes: smelt, sculpin, other bait fish;
birds: coots, terns, pelicans;
probing shorebirds: whimbrel, godwit, willet, sandpiper,

sanderling, stilt, plover, avocet; gulls;
longjaw mudsucker is a fish; mullet, sticklebeck.

Enteromorpha mats: algae.

Not a port.

Up State Street,
train,
winery,
books,
galleries / art museum,
zoo,
university.

Full moon, Venus next to it.

Mountains, ranches,
money can buy.

A hush.
Ceaseless sea
can quell—all—
hush—

Big Book of Birds

topography of song

covert   spurious wing

Dove

pearl diver can be said to have dived
into the girl where she is a girl

the rock dove was introduced into America by the Europeans
a rock is not a pearl although the latter
may be built around the former

these doves carry messages
which is different from rendering unto her
that which is hers

if a message transfers something like a poem
when transported by a girl
                    dove

lark's tongues
her tongue   or tongues

symbolizes peace
        or at least negotiation
a girl is a piece
a repetitive billing
        perhaps at a rate
and cooing
        coo-a-roo
        coo-roo-coo

cock-a-war
coo-cock-cock

repetitive like a poem or a girl

feeds, trusting

established exotic
pinking iridescence
    but the innermost
    no hope
nearly extirpated from overhunting
walks quickly away unless pressed

Sparrow

passerine
    swallow
starling
chestnut crown

long introductory notes
chip
    sweet sweet sweet
        seep
each successive song differs

the male hands the female a twig or grass stem,
which she holds

displays while swaggering on the ground, tail spread
—distraction display—

build in the rain
     glean

conspicuous
bouncing ball trill
high bell-like song
tinkling twitters

hops
feigned injury (when threatened)

jumbled series of phrases
with a seesaw rhythm

Swallow

to devour, swill
to pass through the mouth
     by a series
     of muscular pumping actions
engulf
envelop

Hummingbird

     Susan Howe, *The Liberties*

with—swift—renamed

articulate (connect)
     the rapid vibration of their wings
swoops, dashes, sudden stops and starts

sing
small, small
brilliance and ornamentation rarely rivaled
    rara avis
gorget, crest, pantaloons

Swift

worm or bird
Martin or... fast
scarcely visible   wild screams

know him by this sign
flying anchor, aloft, rarely alight
indirect position of words
    intended
    desire

Nightingale Girl

reposed, inclined, allowed
    posed   aloud
    red
and nightly liking place
    light   spot

For love fingers closed,
    antagonism in sleep
    matter

recovering where
oblivion arrested
    Tsvetaeva, Akhmatova

a girl became a nightingale
mockingbird in America
not a jeweled bird in a gold cage, in clockwork
     in China
the girl music box
she contains the night voice
     stream
polyglottos "many tongued"
dreams
     songs   denuded   Sycamores
in the starry night sky above red carpet
     diplomacy, protocol
where the red dye
the red china
     white house

it is a red tongue
     pink
     bud
     polyp
     hydra, many headed
        salt (sea) kills
        Salton Sea   strong sea
        inland
        a mistake
who cares about men and their matters
          war

the nightingale girl
asked no one
and nothing in particular

this bird imitates dozens of birds
    she poets
as well as animals
    insects
    flies, dragonflies, butterflies
    bees
    spiders
    ants
    beetles
machinery
    hardware
    software
    wetware
    pipes, conduit, chips
    backhoes, piledrivers, steamshovels
even musical instruments
    mandolin
    balalaika
    ukulele
    banjo

I have an object fetish.
she   [insert
poet   a song]
nightingale
bird

sparring *rusticate the numbers*
model / rival teaches
    perches to sing
    a variety of disturbed habitats:
        (southern cross)   x
    suburbia.

Sticks
stems
bits of fabric
dead leaves
string
lined with finer materials
set in a fork
not a spoon
or a knife
or moon

I have an evening whisper song
while sleeping
(drool, chew the pillow, gnash or grind
thousands of dollars of orthodontia
crowns
bleach trays)
I sleep alone.

Call is a *check*.
            x
Two dollar chuck is a bold, abrasive red.
                    wine glut
At night light cough medicine, for health.
                        to song.
                        magic
                                elixir
flutters and tumbles while singing
perches to sing
        to screw a little thing I have
        no girls, phones, or typewriters

May sing well (into the night).
May sing by the glow of a security light
                    (motion sensitive)
                    all night
                    dreamtime on the patio
                    Los Angeles

Girl Mockingbird

...vanish of the moon...
...charming nights when...
...delicate ladies with ripped-off panties,
        mouths open to kiss...

posed, which mouths
        witch
telescope, telephoto, filmy bits
and sleep starts another story,
directed, to be annotated
        subtitled

The Dead
epiphany *Twelfth Night*
a bright light, the star
wise / men / we / follow / why?

what is the voice source?

she is the voice source
is she the foundation
                    fundament
                    fountain
                    youth

she repeats
sequencing
     echoic
(source of) voice what wind
sore
what hole, what jar
mail-ordered
or reality, machine or man or

recovering, the kleptomaniac's mementoes,
          music box
          cage
          china shoe
          limoges
               in the shape of...

uccello notturno
night bird's call

she contains the white bird
     dove / peace
     paloma blanca
     wet &
     white & swift

random trees falling   salt makes sweet seem sweeter skin

To Cry Out

Hoarse after years of this calling,
hours of screams,
swallowing
             tears

persecuted, shot, poisoned, bombed out
             to follow, to sequence, the warrior (carrion)
                        the harvest (corn)
             having chased away doves and mockingbirds

oppressed

the crowd crows over babies cooing, braggadocio wedding
announcements, weddings, raves and exclaims over the job
of the exalted eldest son, new hat, specific Sunday dress or
choice to have a lack of style, outfits miraculously scavenged,
borrowed, collaged together for the rave, clever but never
shockingly original,

which separates one raven from the rest, from the rookery,
the slummy nest, bodies pressed together in their beds, in the
subway, in black cars with tinted windows bumper to bumper
on the black-topped thruway, steaming, honking,

a chicken in every pot, a small defeat to eat, female and
cloaked in one of a closetful of black suits, powerful not chic,
in a consulting firm, small, a bird no one consults, a shrew, a
shrike, a common crow among swindlers and cheats, careless
crackling grackles and jackdaws,

no crow escapes the cooperative flock, the status quo incapable
of wobbling, moving along the z axis, only able to occupy,
densely, that cry,

I am tame, quick to learn, can count and solve puzzles, learn
symbols, retain information.

Eats the eggs of songbirds.

The Wren, The Wren, The Wren

brown
          bird
little   -le
          birdy
               la
               there
hop hop Christmas glistening
ice-glazed trees
trees inside dark green
paneling

Partridge

parturition, to begin to imp
                         art
                operation
the opera of—not fate, not sin—
the democracy of error, inchoate
                mock
for another moment, instant, while
             my
is that mystery, what precedes incunabula?

of thee I sing, that which begins the interminable?
and poetry
                    try
bird poems

Flamingo

abruptly turned down
sheets
to South Beach
flaming-hot
      tropical   color
flamingo clouds

songs on voices birds
instantly recognizable

Heron

from here on in
bittern, solitary,
       with hawks and heron slain

egret, endless display, on platforms,
elaborate movements
        stalk, stab, quawk
        stride, spear
        bill-snapping

blood curdling plumage
even walk resounds

Ibis

decurved, afoul
threskeia, bill a little scythe
    sensitive, to search
gwe gwe, scarlet blown in from Africa
    accidental
croo, croo, white, stylized
daughters pink

wading in
sacred, burned

Stork   stiff
        rigid
        stark

Curlew courier, messenger, run

Tufted Puffin

distinguished   odd-looking
unmistakable   nomadic

silent at sea   dives
for prey

Screech Owl

one she struggles with
buoyant silent flying
rapid wing beats
applause

rapid, shallow   no one beats her
alternate short sliding performance

**Nut-
hatch**

nimble bird   wow
the real   arrived

unique strategy

Woodpecker

noisy
conspicuous
ubiquitous

tongue skewers

in a dead tree with a rotten core
in a fire-blackened snag in an old burn,
stubs broken 10, 20 feet in the air

high I
Q

Art Art Art

Is art
communication?

Landscape Architecture

    Q: What's a vista but a frame?
    Q: What's an exterior room?
    Q: What're these shrubberies?

    A: Here is the box, and outside it.
    A: Here is a gazebo in the arboretum.
    A: Here is your teacher, nature.

    Landscape is situation.
    Pedestrian and vehicular circulation
      situate
        sweet disorder,

    like teaching, the ultimate collaboration.

    See
    signage,
      saw
    potential.

Is art a way?
A truth?
A light-
    well?

                (I know where bungalow heaven is.)

Architecture

From the primitive hut, hearth and therefore heart. Or
heat. At least the Schindler Kings Road House "responds
to the unique climate of Southern California."

I read at a desk inside "the Park they call La Brea," write
on a pad "From the desk of..." and drive along San
Vicente and the ripped-up red car route to you, here,
in this built-in-the-20s-to-look-built-*then* room,
to orthographic,
    axiometric,
    isometric modeling
and a solid code vocabulary

vocalized, transmitted, shouted from the rooftops of
Chiat / Day, Bradbury,
proclaimed from the Walk of Fame:
plans to unfold in space nested inside instructor's
    luncheon, salmon, chicken, salad, on a plate, on a
    cloth, on a table, on a floor, founded on a faultline,

privileged: this fearsome huddle against "the storm," slide,
    inevitable conflagration, tide of Angelinos and time

in which hand, head, and heart move likewise.

It's not all grading and drainage.

Does art
merely
decorate?
Is art a standard
superimposed? On what?

Interior Design

If color affects mood, and so, light, perception,
let's begin our lessons on color, chartreuse to mauve,
    azure's exaltation to puce's profundity.
Let's applaud suede's persuasive suavity,
indeed all texture's rhetoric,
material's culture, and measure
juxtaposition's effects on aesthetics without vexing "the
mix."

Basic / connoisseurship trains the eye,
and vision, trained, discerns.

You have shown the accomplishments of arrangement
and
    demonstrated them.
Tell us (I know you know) ASID designees,

    how is this room doing?

What constraints
does art impose?
Why is Venus here
unclothed? Art controls
and exposes.

Studio Arts

A flower is never really a flower.
A rose...
a cigar...

a painter is not a mirror. A painting is more than paint and
   canvas.
Every great painting leaves.

If an earthquake rips concrete and postmodern tesserae,
   can art's illusion shatter,
invite lovely nightcrawlers to invade uninstructed
   laboratory with models, to pervade ideal and real with
   dream vision, romance,

vine charcoal, brush, wash, ink thrown over paper, awash,
   like the beach with weeds, that is, beauty and terror,
   action and action painting,

lights, camera, super 8,

and a special offering, knowledge, a jewel tone, learning in a
   setting of continuation, extension.

How do artists go,
if not transported
by craft?

Writing

A dynamic character might hula, here,

allowing eternity emerge before slings and flaming arrows
puncture errors in this prose, er, verse, er, ongoing
motivation or plot we call Los Angeles, or speech, or art.
"Ease in writing comes from art, not chance, / as those
move easiest who've learned to dance."

We're not cameras.

Meanwhile, art's history continues   *The author's dead.*
to fade in, fade out.   *Try art.*

Back at the ranch, aliens land,
but they've neither dialogue nor iamb.

They'll learn to talk the talk, walk the walk.
They'll get the nuts and bolts.

I'll be story. You be funny.
Here's the three act-structure: beginning, intermediate,
    advanced punching, comic twisting like we did last
    summer, intensive bible study.
The five: cute meet, pining section, car chase, climax,
    final reveal.

Is life graphic?
Is life
art?

Computer and Graphic Design

Not an auto, not a cad,
no camera tracks an eye across a page,
directs
    reading.
Typography, psychology,
    cultural aesthetics
scale shapes, add emphatic oomph, animate, weave dream
bang, smack
into real world and logos, motion and package, history and
    illustrious example.

Art's illusion cannot shatter;
art controls
and exposes.

Photography

Options in chemistry and in class,
development for better negatives and living,

black-and-white papers and black and white,
foreground and background,   *If, lacking art, brutality reigns,*
Watts Towers and depiction, description thereof,
                            question authority.

Magic of which dreams are made, and
stark fear on milk cartons,

filters, archives,
sequenced, edited,
one's own memory, cultural memory, one's own mind
and making, and finishing.

Do You Hear What I Hear?

said the person of lower rank to the person of higher rank,
the inanimate to the animate, the despot to the populace,

"you don't know what I know, so I'll make you know;
I'll tell you, not show."

It
who   he speaks "holiday"
came upon, on, during, ran across
a clear midnight   midwinter
glorious song of old
an old song, a song about the olden days
                 lore   days of yore
a sunshine holiday
      holy day, batman
holy-tree   holly   like of each thing that in season grows
            heart, fonder
                  most loving mere folly
                  Hollywood Swinging   star
a set, a series of songs of
a holiday like all the holidays
            itself
       like this holiday in the past
used to be (was).
       That is, selectively recall
                  election
            occasion as a memory vehicle
                  poem
Formerly, I knew the season's spirit, this intimate "you."

I'm dreaming, writing, thinking of one color
            with every line I write
                  crib

    manger, manage
this winter "season" was, and I'm anticipating
   time
a winter festival of a different color
   when you aren't with me.

On a clear night
the song arrives: *listen my friends*
hey, listen to what I say
hey, listen, the ones who say "hey" say
      listen sing

pah rum pah pum pum
Do you hear what I hear?
Hardly drums of war.
     War is a ruffian...Plunders God's world of beauty;
     rends away. Christmas tells us the invisible
     horror of the war impinges and disrupts the
     visible world.
sleep in heavenly peace
This poem, this way writing
   saved you. Don't worry about a thing.
From now on, we won't see our troubles.
    They are very distant.
Give us victory o'er the grave a mute Christmas
grave where English oak and holly festoon silent night
and laurel wreathes entwine garland
   wreathe the rod of criticism
encircle weave knit lace plait ornament surround
curls many a wanton wreath I sent you
in hopes that there it could not wither
    an emblem of that mystic charm
the magic of your beauties bind my captive soul

I'm going to say the weather outside is bad even if some might
    call it a land of wonder
and I hope it stays the way I'm pretending it is because I prefer
    it here   California
so I hope I can stay where I am
    with you here, in this poem
as we used to be.

I heard bells and thought it isn't like Christmas used to be—of
ice and snow—I am
in the world I make reborn a stranger.
Who's child is this? *Ooooh, sweet child o' mine.*
    poem
            song

Angels said the first noel, or they said *that* the first noel, wild
    and sweet,
words repeat
it
what has been said many times, many ways:
heaven and heaven and nature sing.

Hook & Ornament

O come
all you
o come
you o come
      (adorn you)

                    o
               Christmas
           tree tree tree
        baum baum kugel
        kugel baum baum
          weihnachten
              tannen
               nacht
               night
                fir
                 o

Here you come,
here you come, right down
the lane.
       (jingle)

                    o
                Babel's
             beaux bows,
          baubles, belles
        lettres, bawdy stories,
  bibliographies, bubbly imbibed, burbling,
    tongues tumult, embellishment
              bell
              bell
               o

Oh, what fun it is to ride.
　　　　　(laughing)

　　　　　　　　　　　　　　o
　　　　　　　　　　　glocke glass
　　　　　　　　　glancing glissando
　　　　　　　gleam glint flash & glitter
　　　　　glockenspiel spiel slang harangue
　　　　　　　persuade, play, peal, *ha,*
　　　　　　　　ha, ha, glisten, listen,
　　　　　　　　　　　clock
　　　　　　　　　　　　&

You're coming to town.
How still we see it lie.
　　　　　(adore you)

　　　　　　　　　　　　&
　　　　　　　　　star, jester's
　　　　　trinket, trifle, in an Ethiope's ear
　　　　　　ornamental　　oriental
　　　　　　　　orare,　ornare

We wish,
we wish, we wish
　　　　(heav'n and nature sing)

It's beginning to look a lot like an occasion.

Catherine Daly was a disk and video jockey in high school in Illinois and college in Connecticut. Her shows were devoted to cover, sample, mix, and mash of noise, novelty, and song. During commutes in California, she began listening to even more recorded poetry and to commercial radio. Her lifelong magpie habits are somewhat legitimized by her work as a general contractor specializing in restoration and her early work in her mother's used clothing stores.

She is author of *DaDaDa* (Salt, 2003), in which song serves memory; *Locket* (Tupelo, 2005), love poems; *To Delite and Instruct* (blue lion, 2006), a meditation on writing exercises and "sounding out"; *Paper Craft* (Moria, 2006), first of a crafts series; *Chanteuse / Cantatrice* (factory school, 2007), a backwards and forwards book about political collaboration, women's writing, and meaning.

www.ingramcontent.com/pod-product-compliance
Lightning Source LLC
Chambersburg PA
CBHW022200080426
42734CB00006B/515